Key Stage 2 Maths

WORKBOOK 6

Numerical Reasoning Technique

Dr Stephen C Curran
with Katrina MacKay

Edited by Andrea Richardson

This book belongs to

Accelerated Education Publications Ltd

Contents

9. Money & Costs   Pages

1. Units of Currency   3
2. Pounds & Pence   3-6
3. Greater Than or Smaller Than   7
4. Coinage   8-17
5. Addition   18-21
6. Subtraction   21-24
7. Multiplication   25-29
8. Division   29-34
9. Money in Words   34-35
10. Problem Solving   35-38

10. Measurement

1. Metric Measurements   39-48
2. Fractions of Measurement   48-50
3. Decimal Measurements   50-52
4. Reading Metric Scales   52-58
5. Greater Than or Smaller Than   58-59
6. Metric Calculations   59-60
7. Estimating Measurements   61-63
8. Temperature   63-65
7. Problem Solving   65-66

11. Averages

1. Mode   67-68
2. Median   68-69
3. Range   69-70
4. The 'Mean' or Average   71-72
5. Problem Solving   72

© 2016 Stephen Curran

Chapter Nine
MONEY & COSTS
1. Units of Currency

Currency is a system of money. The United Kingdom uses pounds and pence as its currency. It is based on the Tens Number System (units of ten).

The basic units of currency are pounds and pence.

Pounds are written as **£**.

Pence are written as **p**.

£1 coin   1p coin

There are **one hundred pence** in **one pound**.

$$100p = £1$$

The pound sign (**£**) is written before the number of pounds. The pence sign (**p**) is written after the number of pence. The signs are never used at the same time.

The decimal point is used to separate the pounds (whole ones) from the pence (less than a whole one).
For example, **£1.60** is **1 pound and 60 pence**.

2. Pounds & Pence

As there are **100 pence** in **one pound**, each penny is worth **one-hundredth** of a pound. This means when pounds and pence are written together using the **£** sign, the pence will only ever be two decimal places. For example:

180p can be written as **£1.80**

23p can be written as **£0.23**

7p can be written as **£0.07**

a. Changing Pounds to Pence

Example: Write **£4.06** as pence.

Step 1 - To change pounds to pence, multiply by **100**. Move the decimal point two places to the right.

$$4.06 \times 100 = 406.0 = 406$$

Step 2 - Change the symbol from **£** to **p**.

Answer: **406p**

Exercise 9: 1 Write as pence:

Score

1) £0.05 = _____
2) £1.99 = _____
3) £5.19 = _____
4) £1.76 = _____
5) £2.30 = _____
6) £0.45 = _____
7) £2.38 = _____
8) £1.20 = _____
9) £3.51 = _____
10) £4.24 = _____

b. Changing Pence to Pounds

Example: Write **130p** as pounds.

Step 1 - To change pence to pounds, divide by **100**. Move the decimal point two places to the left. Remember, a whole number can have a decimal point, so **130** can be written as **130.0**.

$$130.0 \div 100 = 1.30 = 1.30$$

Step 2 - Change the symbol from **p** to **£**.

Answer: **£1.30**

Exercise 9: 2 Write as pounds:

1) **836p** = _____
2) **150p** = _____
3) **299p** = _____
4) **25p** = _____
5) **122p** = _____
6) **308p** = _____
7) **531p** = _____
8) **183p** = _____
9) **74p** = _____
10) **10p** = _____

c. Writing Money in Full

Example: Write **£3.92** as pounds and pence.

Step 1 - The digits to the left of the decimal point are the pounds. There are **3** pounds.

Step 2 - The digits to the right of the decimal point are the pence. There are **92** pence.

Answer: **3 pounds and 92 pence**

Exercise 9: 3 Write as pounds and pence:

1) **£1.53** is _____ pound(s) and _____ pence.
2) **£0.41** is _____ pound(s) and _____ pence.
3) **£2.79** is _____ pound(s) and _____ pence.
4) **£5.63** is _____ pound(s) and _____ pence.
5) **£0.98** is _____ pound(s) and _____ pence.
6) **£3.25** is _____ pound(s) and _____ pence.

© 2016 Stephen Curran

7) £1.81 means ____ pound(s) and ____ pence.

8) £0.67 means ____ pound(s) and ____ pence.

9) £2.30 means ____ pound(s) and ____ pence.

10) £1.07 means ____ pound(s) and ____ pence.

d. Writing Money in Figures

Example: Write **two pounds and thirty-seven pence** in figures.

Two pounds comes before the decimal point and **thirty-seven pence** comes after the decimal point.

Write **£** before the figures.

Answer: **£2.37**

Exercise 9: 4   Write in figures:

1) **Two pounds and eighty-four pence** is _____ .

2) **One pound and twenty-six pence** is _____ .

3) **Zero pounds and fifty-six pence** is _____ .

4) **Four pounds and seventy-five pence** is _____ .

5) **One pound and three pence** is _____ .

6) **One pound and eighty pence** is _____ .

7) **Zero pounds and ninety pence** is _____ .

8) **Five pounds and fourteen pence** is _____ .

9) **Three pounds and thirty-two pence** is _____ .

10) **Zero pounds and one pence** is _____ .

3. Greater Than or Smaller Than

Remember when comparing the size of amounts:
  The sign < means 'smaller than'.
  The sign > means 'bigger than'.
The open end of the sign always faces the larger amount.

Example: Put the correct sign (> or <) between the amounts.
  £3.24   342p

Step 1 - Change the amounts into pence.
  £3.24 is **324p** and **342p** is already in pence.

Step 2 - Compare the size of the amounts and insert the correct sign.
  324p is smaller than **342p**.
  324p < 342p

Step 3 - Change the amounts back to the way they were written in the question.
  Answer: £3.24 < 342p

Exercise 9: 5 Put the correct sign (> or <) between the amounts:

Score

1) £1.36   £1.56   2) 98p   89p

3) £2.76   178p   4) 56p   £0.58

5) £4.54   544p   6) £3.12 302p

7) 18p   £0.81   8) 132p   £1.02

9) £7.00   7p   10) 72p   £1.72

4. Coinage

There are eight commonly used **Coins** in the United Kingdom. The values of each coin can be combined to make any amount.

a. Counting Coins

Example: What is the total value of these coins?

Write the value of each coin and add them together.

£2 + 20p + 5p + 1p = **£2.26**

Answer: **£2.26**

Exercise 9: 6

What is the total value of these coins?

Score

1)   = _____

2)      = _____

3)    = _____

4)    = _____

5)   = _____

6)    = _____

7) 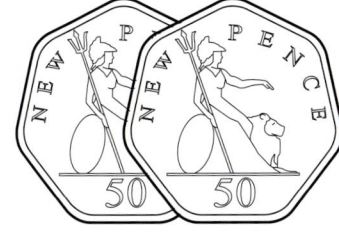   = _____

© 2016 Stephen Curran

8)  = _____

9) 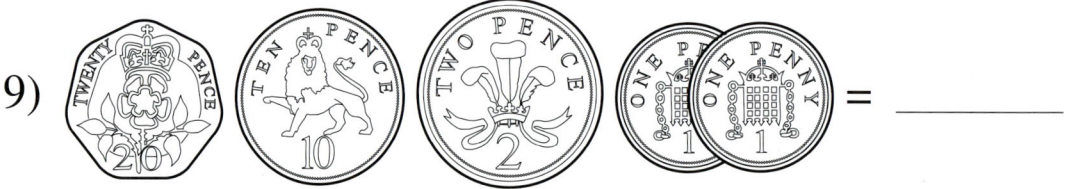 = _____

10)  = _____

b. Missing Coin

Example: These coins should make **50p**. Which coin is missing?

Step 1 - Write the value of each coin and add them together.

20p + 10p + 10p + 2p + 2p + 1p = 45p

Step 2 - Find the coin that needs to be added to **45p** to make **50p**. It is **5p**.

45p + 5p = 50p

Answer: **5p**

Exercise 9: 7

Which coin is missing to make the amount?

Score

To make **10p**:

1) [5p] = _____

2) [5p] [2p] [1p] [1p] = _____

3) [5p] [1p] [1p] [1p] = _____

To make **20p**:

4) [10p] [5p] = _____

5) [5p] [5p] [5p] [2p] [1p] = _____

6) [5p] [2p] [2p] [1p] = _____

To make **50p**:

7) [20p] [10p] = _____

8) [20p] [10p] [5p] [5p] = _____

9) 20p 20p 5p 2p 1p = _____

10) 20p 20p 5p = _____

c. Missing Coins

Example: Find the missing coins to make up **75p**.

75p = 50p + ___ + ___ + ___

The coins must make the value of **75p**. There is already **50p**, so the missing coins must make up the value of **25p**.

Three coins must be used to make this amount.

This must be **10p + 10p + 5p = 25p**.

Answer: **75p = 50p + 10p + 10p + 5p**

Excrcise 9: 8 Fill in the gaps with missing coins to make up these amounts:

Score

1) **48p** = 20p + ____ + ____ + ____ + ____

2) **213p** = £2 + ____ + ____ + ____

3) **150p** = £1 + ____ + ____ + ____

4) **96p** = 50p + ____ + ____ + ____ + ____

5) **52p** = 20p + ____ + ____ + ____

6) **127p** = £1 + ____ + ____ + ____

7) **375p** = **£2** + ____ + ____ + ____ + ____

8) **90p** = **50p** + ____ + ____ + ____

9) **416p** = **£2** + ____ + ____ + ____ + ____

10) **130p** = **5p** + ____ + ____ + ____

d. Least Number of Coins

Example: Which coins make up **37p**, using the least number of coins?

Begin with the largest value of coin that will fit into **37p**, then work down the coin values to make up the amount.

The largest coin is **20p**, followed by **10p**, then **5p** and **2p**. Add the values along the way.

$$20p + 10p + 5p + 2p = 37p$$

Answer: **20p, 10p, 5p and 2p**

Exercise 9: 9 Which coins make up the amount, using the least number of coins?

Score

1) **101p** = ____ ____

2) **75p** = ____ ____ ____

3) **250p** = ____ ____

4) **180p** = ____ ____ ____ ____

5) **408p** = ____ ____ ____ ____ ____

© 2016 Stephen Curran

6) **505p** = _____

7) **83p** = _____

8) **98p** = _____

9) **388p** = _____

10) **312p** = _____

e. Finding Change in Amounts

Example: What change would be given from **£1** if **23p** was spent?

A number line can help show the leftover amount.

Step 1 - Count **2** tens along the number line, then count **3** units, making **23**.

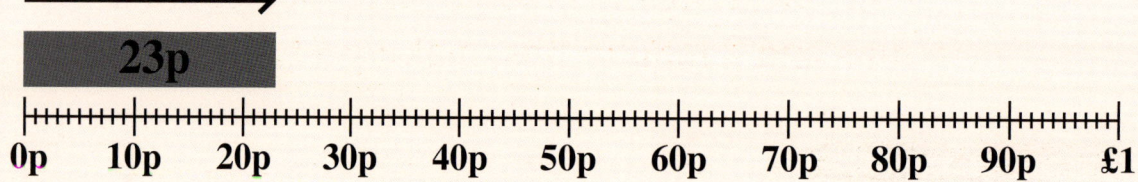

Step 2 - Count back **7** tens from **£1** to get to **30p**. Then count **7** units to get to **23p**. This makes **77p** change.

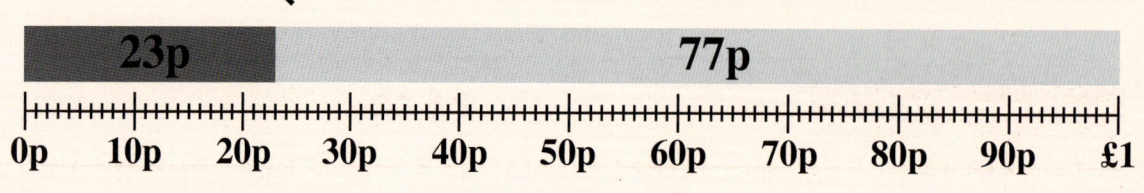

Answer: **77p**

Exercise 9: 10 How much change would be given from £1 if this amount was spent?

Score

|—————|—————|—————|—————|—————|—————|—————|—————|—————|—————|
0p   10p   20p   30p   40p   50p   60p   70p   80p   90p   £1

1) **82p** _____ 2) **13p** _____

3) **56p** _____ 4) **29p** _____

5) **1p** _____ 6) **94p** _____

7) **60p** _____ 8) **58p** _____

9) **35p** _____ 10) **48p** _____

Example: What change would be given from £5 if £1.42 was spent?

Step 1 - Count £1 along the number line, then count **4** tenths and **2** hundredths, making **£1.42**.

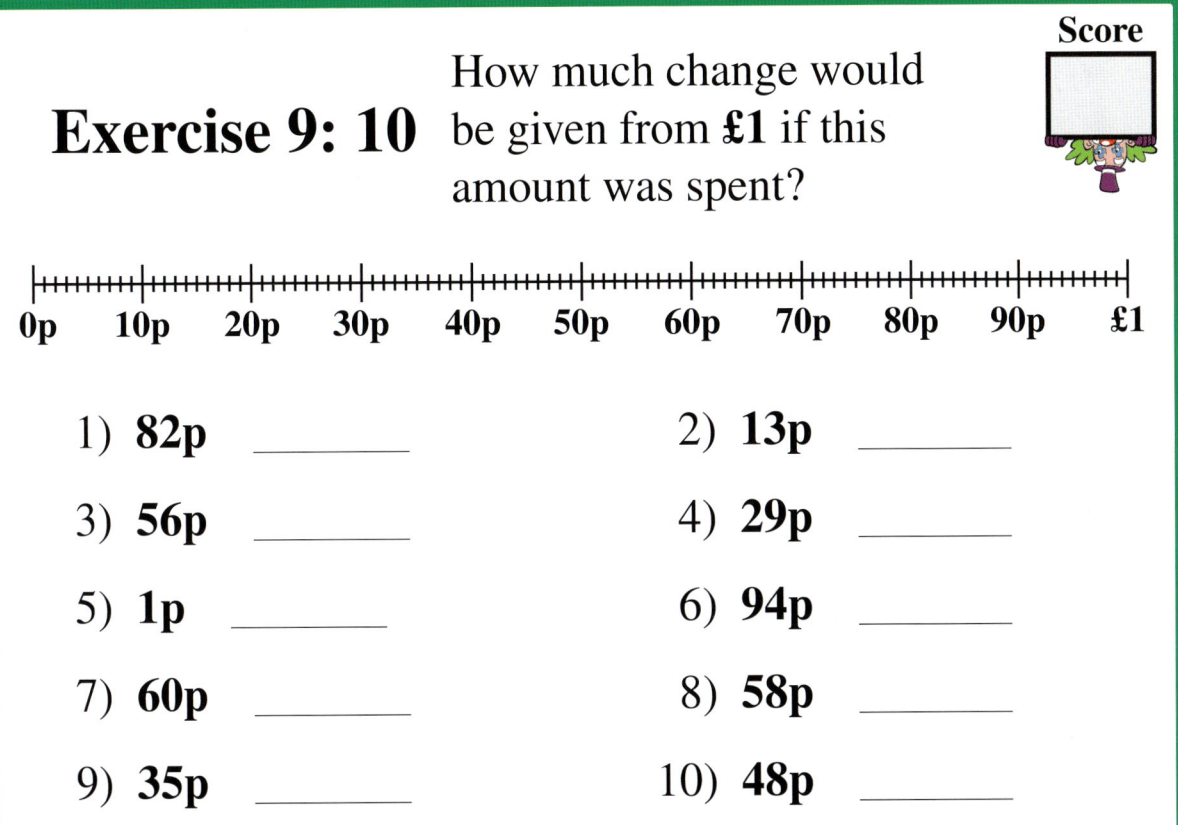

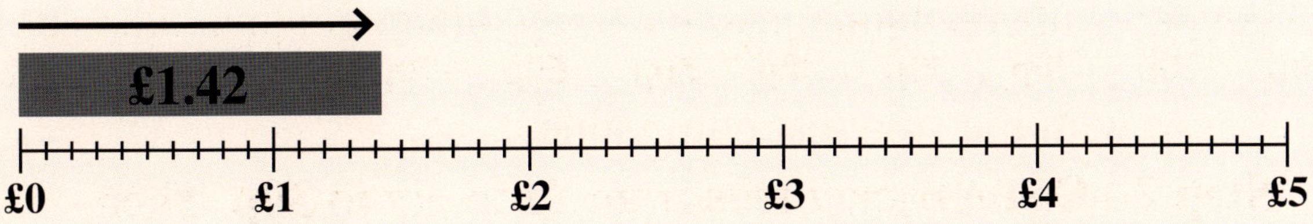

Step 2 - Count back £3 from £5 to get to £2. Then count **5** tenths and **8** hundredths to get to £1.42. This makes **£3.58** change.

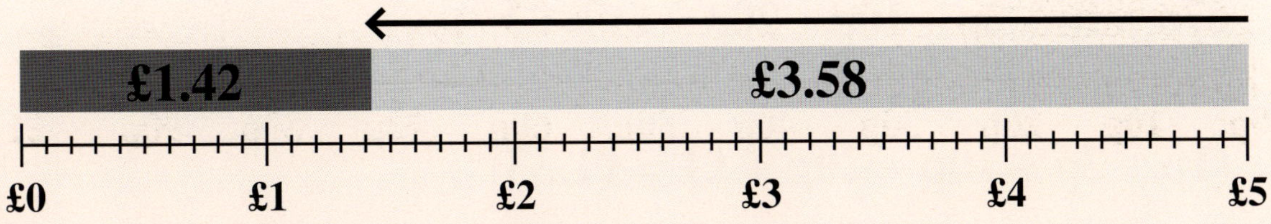

Answer: **£3.58**

© 2016 Stephen Curran

Exercise 9: 11 How much change would be given from **£5** if this amount was spent?

Score

£0 £1 £2 £3 £4 £5

1) £1.18 _____
2) £0.46 _____
3) £2.03 _____
4) £2.75 _____
5) £3.25 _____
6) £0.87 _____
7) £1.70 _____
8) £4.15 _____
9) £3.50 _____
10) £0.92 _____

f. Finding Change in Coins

Example: What change in coins would be given from a **£2** coin if **67p** was spent?

Add the smallest amount of coins to **67p** to make it up to **£2**.

Begin with the smallest coin value, then work up the coin values to make up the amount using the least amount of coins possible.

Add the values along the way.
67p + 1p + 2p + 10p + 20p + £1 = £2
The change is **£1.33**.
(**1p + 2p + 10p + 20p + £1 = £1.33**)

67p + [1p] = 68p
68p + [2p] = 70p
70p + [10p] = 80p
80p + [20p] = £1
£1 + [£1] = £2

Answer: **1p, 2p, 10p, 20p and £1**

Exercise 9: 12

What change in coins would be given if this amount was spent (use the least number of coins)?

Score

From a £1 coin:

1) **26p** = _____

2) **65p** = _____

3) **38p** = _____

From a £2 coin:

4) **£1.03** = _____

5) **78p** = _____

6) **£1.54** = _____

From £5:

7) **£2.67** = _____

8) **£3.41** = _____

From £10:

9) **£5.87** = _____

10) **£8.32** = _____

© 2016 Stephen Curran

5. Addition

The rules for **Adding** money are the same as decimal addition:
1. Keep the decimal points in line.
2. Fill all the empty spaces with **zeros**.
3. Add as normal using standard column addition.

a. Adding Pence

Example: Calculate **61p + 28p + 7p**.

```
  6 1 p
  2 8 p
    7 p +
```

Step 1 - Set out the calculation in column format, keeping the units in line.

Step 2 - Fill in all the empty spaces with **zeros**.

```
  6 1 p
  2 8 p
  0 7 p +
  9 6 p
  1
```

Step 3 - Add as normal.

Answer: **96p**

Exercise 9: 13 Set out and calculate:

Score

1) 37p + 12p

```
  3 7 p
  1 2 p +
  _____
```

2) 49p + 32p

```
  4 9 p
  3 2 p +
  _____
```

3) **56p + 11p**

$$\begin{array}{r} \mathbf{p} \\ \mathbf{p} + \\ \hline \\ \hline \end{array}$$

4) **68p + 5p**

$$\begin{array}{r} \mathbf{p} \\ \mathbf{p} + \\ \hline \\ \hline \end{array}$$

5) **25p + 2p**

$$\begin{array}{r} + \\ \hline \\ \hline \end{array}$$

6) **51p + 26p**

$$\begin{array}{r} + \\ \hline \\ \hline \end{array}$$

7) **67p + 11p + 3p**

$$\begin{array}{r} + \\ \hline \\ \hline \end{array}$$

8) **72p + 15p + 3p**

$$\begin{array}{r} + \\ \hline \\ \hline \end{array}$$

9) **31p + 27p + 18p**

$$\begin{array}{r} + \\ \hline \\ \hline \end{array}$$

10) **89p + 5p + 2p**

$$\begin{array}{r} + \\ \hline \\ \hline \end{array}$$

b. Adding Pounds & Pence

Example: Calculate £14.35 + £2.97.

Step 1 - Set out the calculation in column format, keeping the decimal points in line.

£14.35
£2.97+
_____

Step 2 - Fill in all the empty spaces with **zeros**.

£14.35
£02.97+
_____

Step 3 - Add as normal.

£17.32
 1   1

Answer: **£17.32**

Exercise 9: 14 Set out and calculate:  Score

1) £5.17 + £1.38

£5.17
£1.38+
_____

2) £18.32 + £12.61

£18.32
£12.61+
_____

3) £11.52 + 96p

.
. +
_____

4) £10.52 + £8.16

.
. +
_____

5) £7.63 + £6.12   6) £2.19 + 35p

_____ +   _____ +
_____   _____

7) £36.08 + £12.13 + 98p   8) £9.72 + £4.16 + 52p

_____ +   _____ +
_____   _____

9) £1.26 + £1.11 + 33p   10) £10.74 + £9.20 + £6.03

_____ +   _____ +
_____   _____

6. Subtraction

The rules for **Subtracting** money are the same as decimal subtraction:
1. Keep the decimal points in line.
2. Fill all the empty spaces with **zeros**.
3. Subtract as normal using standard column subtraction.

a. Subtracting Pence

Example: Calculate **50p – 34p**.

$$\begin{array}{r} 5\,0\,p \\ 3\,4\,p\,- \\ \hline \end{array}$$

Step 1 - Set out the calculation in column format, keeping the units in line.

Step 2 - Subtract as normal.

$$\begin{array}{r} {}^4\!\!\!\not{5}\,{}^1 0\,p \\ 3\,4\,p\,- \\ \hline 1\,6\,p \end{array}$$

Answer: **16p**

Exercise 9: 15 Set out and calculate:

Score

1) 75p – 41p

    7 5 p
    4 1 p –
    ———

2) 93p – 17p

    9 3 p
    1 7 p –
    ———

3) 64p – 22p

       p
       p –
    ———

4) 85p – 36p

       p
       p –
    ———

5) 18p – 9p

6) 39p – 26p

7) **95p – 27p**   8) **86p – 13p**

9) **79p – 36p**   10) **65p – 42p**

b. Subtracting Pounds & Pence

Example: Calculate **£11.04 – £6.83**.

Step 1 - Set out the calculation in column format, keeping the decimal points in line.

$$£11.04$$
$$£6.83-$$

Step 2 - Fill in all empty spaces with **zeros**.

Step 3 - Subtract as normal.

$$£{}^0\!\!\!\not{1}{}^1\!\!\!\not{1}.{}^10\,4$$
$$£06.83-$$
$$£04.21$$

Answer: **£4.21**

Exercise 9: 16 Set out and calculate:

Score

1) £1.07 − 32p

  £ 1 . 0 7
  £ 0 . 3 2 −
  ─────────

2) £8.16 − £2.08

  £ 8 . 1 6
  £ 2 . 0 8 −
  ─────────

3) £10.62 − £1.13

4) £28.13 − £6.36

5) £7.86 − £2.19

6) £5.13 − £2.06

7) £25.07 − £8.16

8) £16.99 − £5.12

9) £25.19 − £14.08

10) £36.22 − £12.08

7. Multiplication

Multiplying Money is the same as repeated addition.
For example, **50p × 3 = 50p + 50p + 50p = £1.50**

a. Multiplying Pence

Example: What is the value of these coins?

As there are **seven 5p** coins,
it is quicker to multiply by **7**
than to add up the coins.

5 × 7 = 35, so **5p × 7 = 35p**

Answer: **35p**

Exercise 9: 17   What is the value of:

Score

1)  = _____

2)  = _____

3)  = _____

4)  = _____

5) 🪙🪙🪙 = _____

6) 🪙🪙🪙🪙🪙🪙🪙🪙🪙 = _____

7) 🪙🪙🪙🪙 = _____

8) 🪙🪙🪙 = _____

9) 🪙🪙🪙🪙🪙🪙🪙 = _____

10) 🪙🪙🪙🪙🪙 = _____

Example: Calculate **83p × 5**.

Step 1 - Set out the calculation as a standard short column multiplication.

```
  8 3 p
    5 ×
  _____
```

Step 2 - Multiply as normal. The **4** must be carried into the hundreds column. As there are **100p** in **£1**, insert a decimal point to convert the answer to pounds.

```
  8 3 p
    5 ×
  _____
  £4.15
   4  1
```

Answer: **£4.15**

Exercise 9: 18   Set out and calculate:

Score

1) **76p × 3**

$$\begin{array}{r} 7\,6\,\text{p} \\ 3\,\times \\ \hline \pounds\quad. \\ \hline \end{array}$$

2) **14p × 9**

$$\begin{array}{r} 1\,4\,\text{p} \\ 9\,\times \\ \hline \pounds\quad. \\ \hline \end{array}$$

3) **23p × 5**

$$\begin{array}{r} \text{p} \\ \times \\ \hline \pounds\quad. \\ \hline \end{array}$$

4) **92p × 2**

$$\begin{array}{r} \text{p} \\ \times \\ \hline \pounds\quad. \\ \hline \end{array}$$

5) **38p × 7**

6) **57p × 4**

7) **40p × 6**

8) **81p × 9**

9) **9p × 8**

10) **65p × 7**

b. Multiplying Pounds & Pence

When multiplying money, simply multiply as normal using standard column multiplication. Be careful to write the decimal point and keep it in line in the answer.

Example: Calculate £1.25 × 6.

Step 1 - Set out the calculation as a standard short column multiplication.

```
  £ 1 . 2 5
        6 ×
  ─────────
```

Step 2 - Multiply as normal. Be careful to transfer the decimal point to the answer.

```
  £ 1 . 2 5
        6 ×
  ─────────
  £ 7 . 5 0
      1   3
```

Answer: **£7.50**

Exercise 9: 19 Set out and calculate:

1) £3.21 × 8

```
  3 . 2 1
      8 ×
  ───────
      .
  ───────
```

2) £1.79 × 5

```
  1 . 7 9
      3 ×
  ───────
      .
  ───────
```

3) £7.16 × 2

```
      .
      ×
  ───────
      .
  ───────
```

4) £8.89 × 7

```
      .
      ×
  ───────
      .
  ───────
```

5) £1.02 × 9

6) £5.57 × 6

7) £4.95 × 4

8) £6.73 × 3

9) £9.64 × 2

10) £9.99 × 5

8. Division
a. Dividing Pence

Example: How many **2p** coins are worth **18p**?

Think of how many **2p** coins will make up **18p**.

There are **nine 2p** coins because **2p × 9 = 18p**.

So, **18p** divided by **2p** equals **9**.

Answer: **9**

Exercise 9: 20 Answer the following:

Score

1) How many **2p** coins are worth **22p**? _____

2) How many **2p** coins are worth **16p**? _____

3) How many **5p** coins are worth **40p**? _____

4) How many **5p** coins are worth **55p**? _____

5) How many **10p** coins are worth **80p**? _____

6) How many **10p** coins are worth **30p**? _____

7) How many **10p** coins are worth **50p**? _____

8) How many **20p** coins are worth **80p**? _____

9) How many **20p** coins are worth **40p**? _____

10) How many **50p** coins are worth **£1**? _____

Example: Calculate **78p ÷ 6**.

Step 1 - Set out the calculation as a standard short division.

$$6\overline{)78\,p}$$

Step 2 - Divide as standard short division.

$$6\overline{)7^{1}8\,p} = 13\,p$$

Answer: **13p**

Exercise 9: 21   Set out and calculate:

Score

1) **84p ÷ 4**

2) **96p ÷ 8**

$$4\overline{\smash{)}84\,p}$$

$$8\overline{\smash{)}96\,p}$$

3) **57p ÷ 3**

4) **68p ÷ 2**

5) **99p ÷ 9**

6) **98p ÷ 7**

7) **85p ÷ 5**

8) **96p ÷ 6**

9) **84p ÷ 6**

10) **88p ÷ 8**

b. Dividing Pounds & Pence

Example: How many **20p** coins are in **£5**?

Step 1 - Think of how many **20p** coins will make up **£1**.

There are **five 20p** coins because:

20p × 5 = 100p = £1

Step 2 - Multiply by **5** to work out how many **20p** coins are in **£5**.

5 × 5 = 25 coins

So, if **£5** is divided by **20p**, the answer is **25**.

Answer: **25**

Exercise 9: 22   Answer the following:

1) How many **10p** coins are in **£1**? _____
2) How many **20p** coins are in **£3**? _____
3) How many **20p** coins are in **£6**? _____
4) How many **20p** coins are in **£7**? _____
5) How many **50p** coins are in **£4**? _____
6) How many **50p** coins are in **£2**? _____
7) How many **50p** coins are in **£5**? _____
8) How many **5p** coins are in **£2**? _____
9) How many **2p** coins are in **£1**? _____
10) How many **10p** coins are in **£2**? _____

Score

When dividing money, simply divide as normal using standard short division. Be careful to write the decimal point and keep it in line in the answer.

Example: Calculate £1.59 ÷ 3.

Step 1 - Set out the calculation as a standard short division.

3 | £1.59

Step 2 - Divide, keeping the decimal point in line in the answer.

£0.53
3 | £1.⁵9

Answer: **£0.53**

Exercise 9: 23   Set out and calculate:

1) £2.96 ÷ 8

2) £4.59 ÷ 3

8 | £2.96

3 | £4.59

3) £3.75 ÷ 5

4) £5.88 ÷ 6

5) £7.50 ÷ 2

6) £4.86 ÷ 9

7) £8.20 ÷ 5

8) £9.38 ÷ 7

9) £6.44 ÷ 7

10) £9.36 ÷ 4

9. Money in Words

Below is a reminder of the different words used to describe the Four Rules of Number:

Add	Subtract	Multiply	Divide
Plus	Less	Find the product of	Share
Total	Minus	Multiply	Divide
Increase	Take away/from	Times	Find the quotient
Combine	Deduct	Double/Twice (×2)	Partition
Altogether	Decrease	Treble/Triple (×3)	Separate into
Find the sum of	Find the difference	Quadruple (×4)	Split into

Example: What is the value of **3 five pence pieces** plus **2 twenty pence pieces**?

This calculation involves two stages:

Step 1 - Work out the value of the given amounts.

3 five pence pieces means **5p × 3**, which is **15p**.

2 twenty pence pieces means **20p × 2**, which is **40p**.

Step 2 - 'Plus' is the same thing as using the + sign.

Add the two values together:

15p + 40p = 55p

Answer: **55p**

Exercise 9: 24 Answer the following:

Score

1) Find the product of **3 two pence pieces** and **8 pennies**. _____

2) What is the value of **2 twenty pence pieces** minus **6 pennies**? _____

3) Increase **3 ten pence pieces** by **3 twenty pence pieces**. _____

4) Share **twenty pence** into **4**. _____

5) What is the value of **5 ten pence pieces** plus **3 fifty pence pieces**? _____

6) Find the difference between **3 twenty pence pieces** and **6 two pence pieces**. _____

7) Multiply **2 ten pence pieces** by **4 two pence pieces**. _____

8) Combine **4 fifty pence pieces** with **3 five pence pieces**. _____

9) Divide **4 twenty pence pieces** by **10**. _____

10) Find the sum of **3 two pence pieces**, **2 twenty pence pieces** and **5 five pence pieces**. _____

10. Problem Solving

Money problems use the Four Rules of Number. Level 1 questions require only one operation. Level 2 questions require two operations.

a. Level 1

Example: If a bag of sweets costs **40p**, how many bags can be bought for **£2.40**?

This question can be easily done using repeated addition.
Keep adding **40p** until the correct amount is reached.
Six 40p amounts are added together.

40p + 40p = 80p
80p + 40p = £1.20
£1.20 + 40p = £1.60
£1.60 + 40p = £2.00
£2.00 + 40p = £2.40

Answer: **6**

Exercise 9: 25   Answer the following:

Score

1) A chocolate bar costs **20p**. What is the maximum number of bars Jamie can buy with **£1.80**? _____

2) If burgers cost **£1.95** each, how much will it cost for **5** friends to have a burger each? _____

3) A pen costs **12p**. If a pack of pens costs **£1.20**, how many pens are in the pack? _____

4) A slice of cake costs **25p**. A cake has been cut into **8** slices. How much does the whole cake cost? _____

5) Charlie has **£2.76**, Zach has **£1.22** and James has **58p**. How much money do the children have altogether? _____

6) Jessie buys a packet of crisps. She pays with a **£1** coin and receives **28p** change. How much did the packet of crisps cost? _____

7) Sennah wants to buy a computer game that costs **£20.00**. She is given **£2.50** pocket money each week. For how many weeks will she need to save her money? _____

8) Year 3 are going swimming. There are **35** children and each child has to pay **£3**. How much money must be collected in total? _____

9) Jenna buys a book costing **£7.50**, a top costing **£9.50** and lunch costing **£3.97**. How much did she spend in total? _____

10) Fatimah is given **£18** for lunch for the week. She has **£2.80** left at the end of the week. How much did she spend? _____

b. Level 2

Example: Gurpreet has **£10** to spend. She buys **4** comics. Two comics cost **45p** each. The other two cost **73p** and **99p**. She also buys a pack of stickers for **£3.20**. How much change does she get?

This question has two operations.

Step 1 - Find the total cost of the items bought by adding the amounts.

It is easier to convert all of the amounts to pounds.

The total amount is **£5.82**.

```
  £0.45
  £0.45
  £0.73
  £0.99
  £3.20+
  £5.82
    2 2
```

Step 2 - To find the change, use standard column subtraction from **£10**.

£10.00 – £5.82 = £4.18

```
  £1⁰0.⁹0⁹0¹
  £05.82–
  £04.18
```

Answer: **£4.18**

Exercise 9: 26   Answer the following:

Score

1) John buys **three** books for **£1.25** each. He also buys a notebook for **99p**. How much does he spend in total? _____

2) Coloured pencils cost **35p** per pack of **20**. How much will **100** pencils cost? _____

3) April and her **2** brothers are given **£2.50** each per week. How much will they have altogether after **4** weeks? _____

4) A cup of tea costs **£1.20** and a biscuit costs **50p**. Dad buys **2** cups of tea and **1** biscuit. How much does he spend? _____

5) Heather buys **2** tops and gets **£7.50** change from **£20**. How much did each top cost? _____

6) How much money is in the box? _____

50p	20p	10p	5p	2p	1p
3	2	1	1	2	3

7) Tanya has **£7**. She is given a **£2** coin and a **20p** coin. She wants to reach **£10**. How much more money does she need? _____

8) How much money is in the box? _____

50p	20p	10p	5p	2p	1p
2	2	2	1	3	1

9) Jayne has **£12**. She needs **£15**. If she gets a **£2** coin, how much more money does she need? _____

10) Stickers cost **20p** per pack of **20** stickers. How much do **120** stickers cost? _____

Chapter Ten
MEASUREMENT
1. Metric Measurements

Metric Measurements are based on the Tens Number System. There are four types of measurement:
- **Distance** - the length of something
- **Weight** - how heavy something is
- **Capacity** - how much space is inside something
- **Temperature** - how hot or cold something is

Metric measurements use the following common descriptions. 'Milli' is the smallest and 'kilo' is the largest.

Milli	$\frac{1}{1000}$	One-thousandth
Centi	$\frac{1}{100}$	One-hundredth
Kilo	**1,000**	One Thousand

a. Distance

Distance is the measurement of how long something is. Units of distance measurement from smallest to largest are:
- **millimetres** or **mm**
- **centimetres** or **cm**
- **metres** or **m**
- **kilometres** or **km**

Measurements can be written in, or converted to, any of the above forms. Some important conversions are listed below:

10 millimetres (mm) = **1** centimetre (cm)
1,000 millimetres (mm) = **1** metre (m)
100 centimetres (cm) = **1** metre (m)
1,000 metres (m) = **1** kilometre (km)

© 2016 Stephen Curran

Example: Change **200** centimetres (cm) to metres (m).

Step 1 - Use the distance conversions box to check how many centimetres are in a metre.

100 centimetres (cm) = **1** metre (m)

Step 2 - Multiply by **2** to find **200** centimetres in metres.

$1 \times 2 = 2$

Answer: **2 metres** (or **2m**)

Exercise 10: 1 Calculate the following:

1) **5km** = _____ m
2) **4cm** = _____ mm
3) **300cm** = _____ m
4) **70mm** = _____ cm
5) **20mm** = _____ cm
6) **8,000m** = _____ km
7) **1,000mm** = _____ m
8) **9m** = _____ cm
9) **6,000mm** = _____ m
10) **1km** = _____ m

Distances should be measured in the most suitable unit. Examples of everyday objects are given below for each unit of measurement, making it easier to judge the correct unit:

1 millimetre or **1mm**   **1 centimetre** or **1cm**   **1 metre** or **1m**   **1 kilometre** or **1km**

  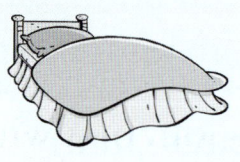 

Roughly the thickness of a credit card.   Roughly the width of a finger.   Roughly the width of a single bed.   Roughly the distance travelled in a 12-minute walk.

Example: Is a rabbit more or less than **1** metre in length?

The length of a rabbit is less than the width of a single bed, so it is less than **1** metre in length.

Answer: **Less than 1 metre**

Exercise 10: 2   Sort the objects into the table below:

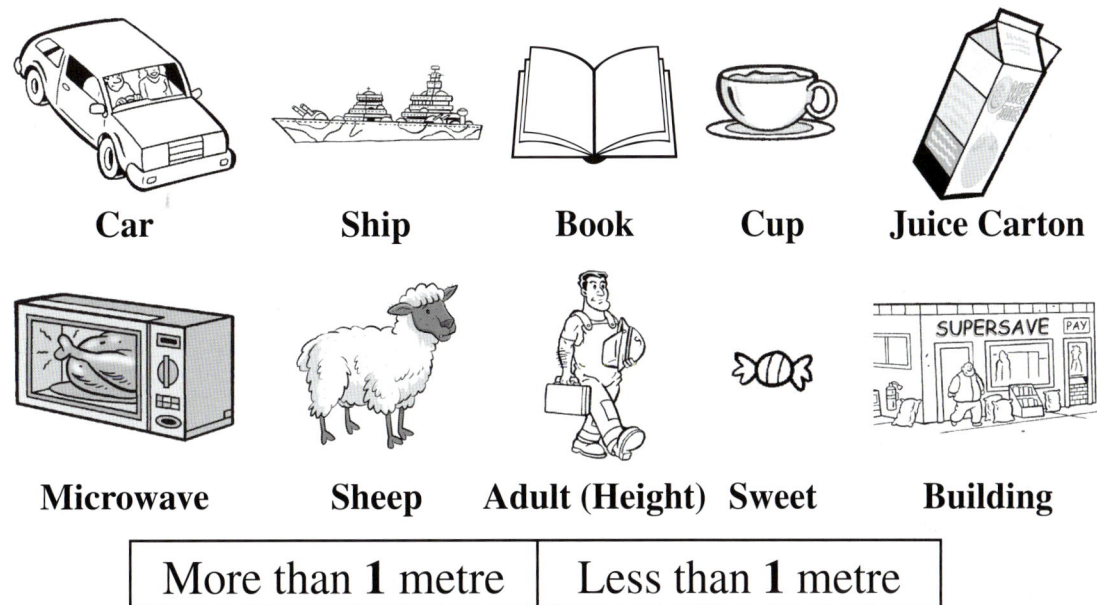

Car   Ship   Book   Cup   Juice Carton

Microwave   Sheep   Adult (Height)   Sweet   Building

More than **1** metre	Less than **1** metre

Score

Example: What unit would be used to measure the width of a whiteboard?

The width of a whiteboard is more than the width of a single bed, so the best unit of measurement is metres (m).

Answer: **metres (m)**

Exercise 10: 3 What unit would be used to measure:

1) the length of a pen? _____
2) the height of a van? _____
3) the width of a desk? _____
4) the length of a ruler? _____
5) the distance between two towns? _____
6) the thickness of a die? _____
7) the length of a folder? _____
8) the thickness of a business card? _____
9) the height of a mountain? _____
10) the length of a piece of paper? _____

Score

b. Weight

Weight is the measurement of how heavy something is.

Units of weight measurement from smallest to largest are:

- **grams** or **g**
- **kilograms** or **kg**
- **tonnes** or **t**

Measurements can be written in, or converted to, any of the above forms. Some important conversions are listed below:

1,000 grams (g)   = **1** kilogram (kg)
1,000 kilograms (kg) = **1** tonne (t)

Example: How many grams (g) are in **3** kilograms (kg)?

Step 1 - Use the weight conversions box to check how many grams are in a kilogram.

1,000 grams (g) = **1** kilogram (kg)

Step 2 - Multiply by **3** to find **3** kilograms in grams.

1,000 × **3** = **3,000**

Answer: **3,000 grams** (or **3,000g**)

Exercise 10: 4   Calculate the following:

1) **8kg** = _____g
2) **5,000g** = _____kg
3) **2kg** = _____g
4) **7,000g** = _____kg
5) **6,000g** = _____kg
6) **9,000g** = _____kg
7) **4kg** = _____g
8) **1,000g** = _____kg
9) **3,000g** = _____kg
10) **1,000kg** = _____t

Weight should be measured in the most suitable unit. Examples of the weights of everyday objects are given below for each unit of measurement, making it easier to judge the correct unit:

1 gram   **1 kilogram**   **1 tonne**
or **1g**   or **1kg**   or **1t**

Roughly the weight of a paperclip.   Roughly the weight of a bag of sugar.   Roughly the weight of a rhinoceros.

Example: Does a mobile phone weigh more or less than **1** kilogram?

The weight of a mobile phone is less than a bag of sugar, so it is less than **1** kilogram in weight.

Answer: **Less than 1 kilogram**

Exercise 10: 5
Sort the objects into the table below:

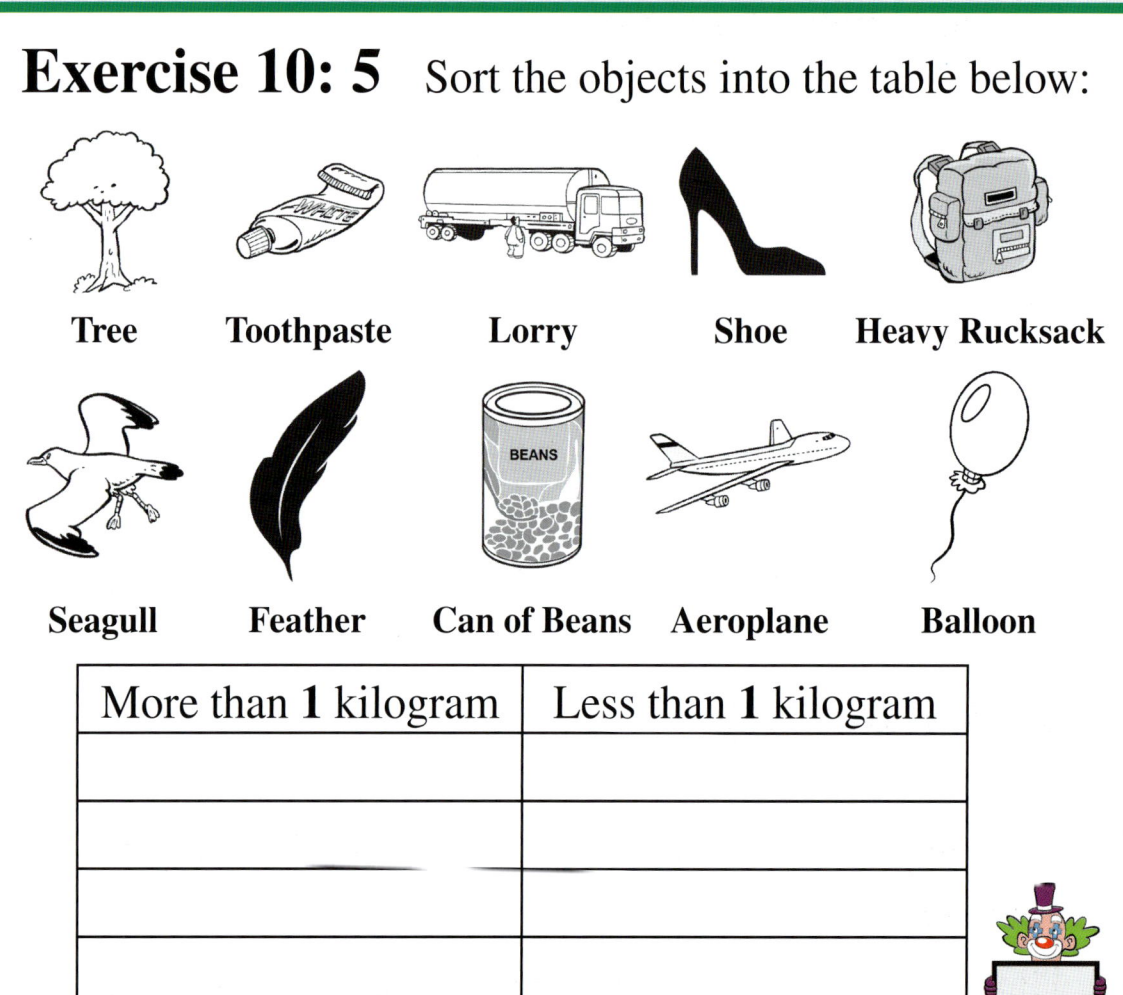

Tree   Toothpaste   Lorry   Shoe   Heavy Rucksack

Seagull   Feather   Can of Beans   Aeroplane   Balloon

More than **1** kilogram	Less than **1** kilogram

Example: What unit would be used to measure the weight of a bus?

The weight of a bus would be more than the weight of a rhinoceros, so the best unit of measurement is tonnes (t).

Answer: **tonnes (t)**

Exercise 10: 6 What unit would be used to measure:

1) the weight of a fire engine? _____

2) the weight of a photograph? _____

3) the weight of a snowball? _____

4) the weight of a person? _____

5) the weight of a hippopotamus? _____

6) the weight of a flag? _____

7) the weight of a full suitcase? _____

8) the weight of a dog? _____

9) the weight of a DVD? _____

10) the weight of a cruise ship? _____

Score

c. Capacity

Capacity is the measurement of how much space is inside something.

Units of capacity measurement from smallest to largest are:

- **millilitres** or **mℓ**
- **litres** or **ℓ**

Measurements can be written in, or converted to, any of the above forms. Some important conversions are listed below:

1,000 millilitres (mℓ) = **1** litre (ℓ)

Example: Convert **4** litres (ℓ) to millilitres (mℓ).

Step 1 - Use the capacity conversions box to check how many millilitres are in a litre.
1 litre (ℓ) = **1,000** millilitres (mℓ)

Step 2 - Multiply by **4** to find **4** litres in millilitres.
1,000 × **4** = **4,000**
Answer: **4,000 millilitres** (or **4,000mℓ**)

Exercise 10: 7   Calculate the following:

1) **1,000mℓ** = _____ ℓ
2) **7,000mℓ** = _____ ℓ
3) **6ℓ** = _____ mℓ
4) **8ℓ** = _____ mℓ
5) **10ℓ** = _____ mℓ
6) **2ℓ** = _____ mℓ
7) **4,000mℓ** = _____ ℓ
8) **9,000mℓ** = _____ ℓ
9) **5,000mℓ** = _____ ℓ
10) **3ℓ** = _____ mℓ

Capacity, or the space inside something, should be measured in the most suitable unit. Examples of the capacity of everyday objects are given below for each unit of measurement, making it easier to judge the correct unit:

1 millilitre or **1mℓ**

1 litre or **1ℓ**

Roughly 20 raindrops in capacity.

Roughly a jug of water in capacity.

Example: Which has a greater capacity, a paddling pool or a wellington boot?

Capacity is how much space is inside something. A paddling pool has more space inside it than a wellington boot, so it has a greater capacity.

Answer: **A paddling pool**

Exercise 10: 8   Circle the object with the greater capacity:

9) Egg Cup   Trophy   10) Vase   Teaspoon

Example: What unit would be used to measure the capacity of a bucket?

The capacity of a bucket would be more than the capacity of a jug, so the best unit of measurement is litres (ℓ).

Answer: **litres (ℓ)**

Exercise 10: 9 What unit would be used to measure:

1) the capacity of a pig's trough? _____

2) the capacity of a jam jar? _____

3) the capacity of a thimble? _____

4) the capacity of a mixing bowl? _____

5) the capacity of a beaker? _____

6) the capacity of a flask? _____

7) the capacity of a glass? _____

8) the capacity of a kettle? _____

9) the capacity of a plant pot? _____

10) the capacity of a teacup? _____

Score

2. Fractions of Measurement

It is useful to know basic fractions of $\frac{1}{4}$, $\frac{1}{2}$ and $\frac{3}{4}$ of distance, weight and capacity measurements.

For example, $\frac{1}{2}$ of **1** metre in centimetres is **50cm**.

The box below is reminder of the main measurements:

Length

1 centimetre (cm) = 10 millimetres (mm)
1 metre (m) = 1,000 millimetres (mm)
1 metre (m) = 100 centimetres (cm)
1 kilometre (km) = 1,000 metres (m)

Weight

1 kilogram (kg) = 1,000 grams (g)
1 tonne (t) = 1,000 kilograms (kg)

Capacity

1 litre (ℓ) = 1,000 millilitres (mℓ)

Example: What is $\frac{3}{4}$ of 1 kilogram in grams?

Step 1 - Change 1 kilogram into grams.

　　　1 kilogram (kg) = 1,000 grams (g)

Step 2 - Find $\frac{1}{4}$ of 1,000 grams by dividing.

　　Divide the whole number by the denominator, which is **4**.
　　　1,000 ÷ 4 = 250

Step 3 - Find $\frac{3}{4}$ by multiplying.

　　Multiply **250** by the numerator, which is **3**.
　　　250 × 3 = 750

　　Answer: **750 grams**

Exercise 10: 10 Calculate the following:

1) What is $\frac{1}{2}$ of **1cm** in millimetres? _____

2) What is $\frac{1}{4}$ of **1ℓ** in millilitres? _____

3) What is $\frac{1}{2}$ of **1kg** in grams? _____

4) What is $\frac{1}{2}$ of **1m** in centimetres? _____

5) What is $\frac{3}{4}$ of **1m** in millimetres? _____

6) What is $\frac{1}{4}$ of **1kg** in grams? _____

7) What is $\frac{1}{2}$ of **1ℓ** in millilitres? _____

8) What is $\frac{1}{2}$ of **1km** in metres? _____

9) What is $\frac{1}{4}$ of **1m** in centimetres? _____

10) What is $\frac{3}{4}$ of **1km** in metres? _____

3. Decimal Measurements

Decimal Measurements can be split into two separate units of measurement.

For example:

  3.5kg could be written as **3** kilograms and **500** grams.

An easy error would be to write this amount as **3** kilograms and **5** grams and not realise that **0.5** is **half** a kilogram and must be written as **500** grams.

Example: Write **1.5ℓ** in litres and millilitres.

Step 1 - The digits to the left of the decimal point can be written as litres. There is **1** litre.

Step 2 - **0.5ℓ** is half of **1ℓ**, which is **500mℓ**.

Answer: **1 litre and 500 millilitres**

Exercise 10: 11 Fill in the equivalent amount:

1) **6.5cm** = _____cm and _____mm
2) **1.75km** = _____km and _____m
3) **3.25kg** = _____kg and _____g
4) **2.5kg** = _____kg and _____g
5) **8.5m** = _____m and _____cm
6) **5.25ℓ** = _____ℓ and _____mℓ
7) **4.75ℓ** = _____ℓ and _____mℓ
8) **7.5m** = _____m and _____cm
9) **9.25kg** = _____kg and _____g
10) **1.25t** = _____t and _____kg

Score

Example: Write **4** kilograms and **750** grams in kilograms.

Step 1 - **4** kilograms is written to the left of the decimal point as **4.0**.

Step 2 - **750g** is **three-quarters** of **1kg**, which would be written as **0.75kg**.

Answer: **4.75 kilograms**

Exercise 10: 12 Fill in the equivalent amount:

1) **1kg and 500g** = _____ kg

2) **3m and 25cm** = _____ m

3) **9ℓ and 750mℓ** = _____ ℓ

4) **7km and 250m** = _____ km

5) **4cm and 5mm** = _____ cm

6) **2cm and 5mm** = _____ cm

7) **5ℓ and 750mℓ** = _____ ℓ

8) **6m and 25cm** = _____ m

9) **1km and 750m** = _____ km

10) **8kg and 250g** = _____ kg

Score

4. Reading Metric Scales
a. Measuring Distance

Rulers are usually marked up in metric units of metres, centimetres and millimetres:

   10 millimetres = **1** centimetre
   100 centimetres = **1** metre

Most rulers, like the one below, are shorter than **1** metre.

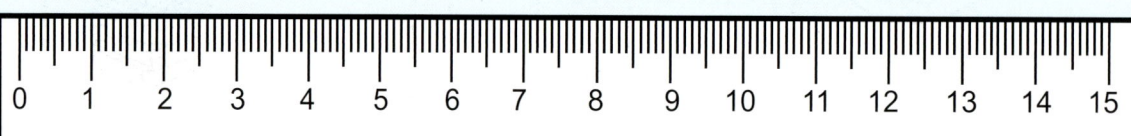

Example: What measurement does the arrow point to on the ruler? Give the answer in centimetres and in millimetres.

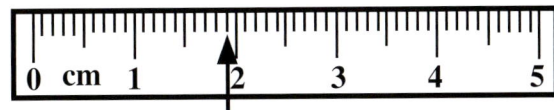

The arrow points to **1cm and 9mm**. This can be written as **1.9cm** or **19mm**.

Answer: **1.9cm** or **19mm**

Exercise 10: 13

What measurements are the arrows pointing to on the ruler?

Score

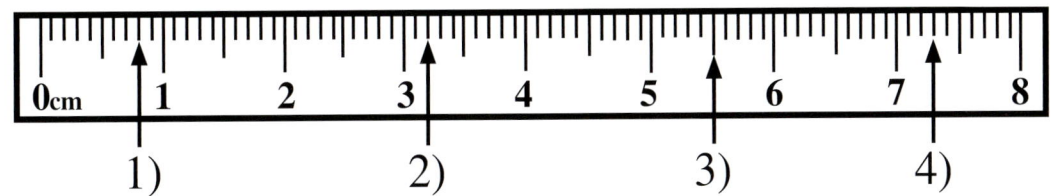

1) _____mm   2) _____cm

3) _____mm   4) _____cm

Use a ruler to measure the following drawings of objects (be careful to measure to the end of the lines):

5)    6) 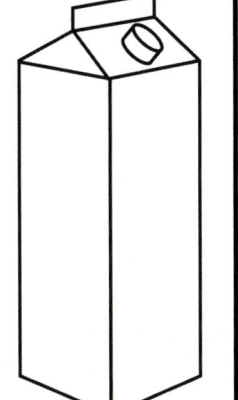   7)

_____   _____   _____

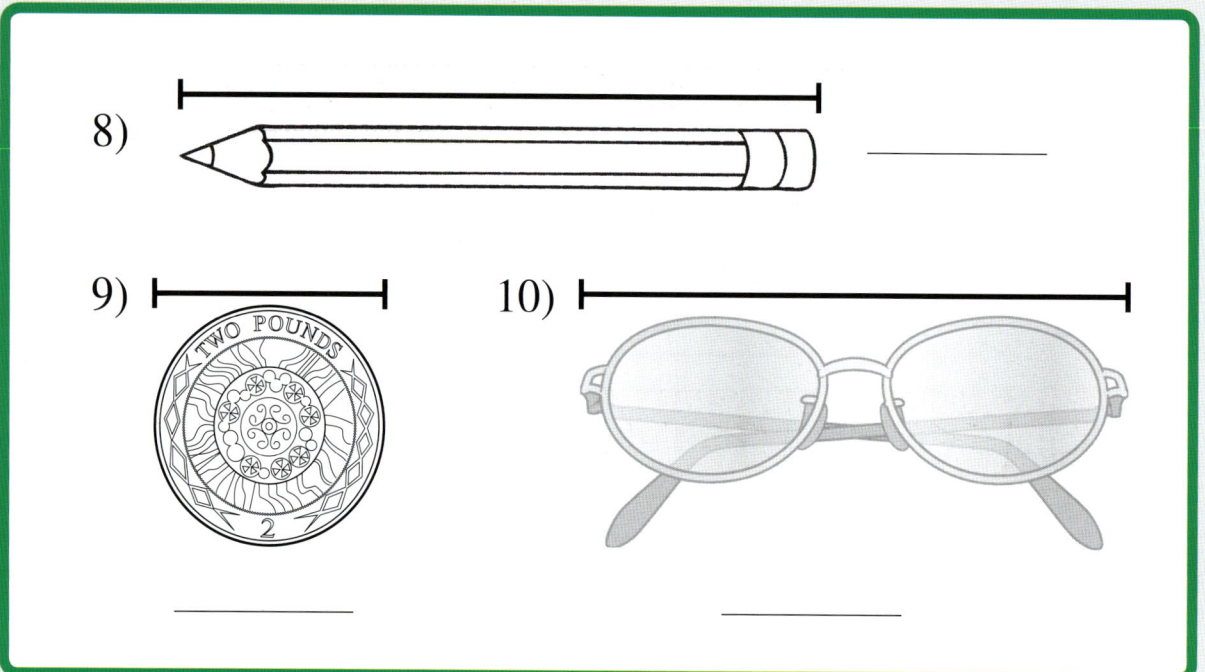

b. Measuring Weight

Scales are used to measure how heavy something is. Balancing scales (pair of scales) are a type of weighing device.

They have a balance beam and two dishes and work in a similar way to a see-saw.

To measure an object's weight, it is placed in one dish and standard weights are placed in the other dish until the scales balance. This means both sides contain exactly the same weight.

Examples of standard weights are shown below:

Example: How many **250g** weights are in **1kg**?

1 kilogram is **1,000** grams, so **four** lots of **250g** will make up **1,000g**, as shown below:

250g + 250g + 250g + 250g = **1kg**

Answer: **4**

Exercise 10: 14 Answer the following:

1) How many **50g** weights are in **100g**? _____

2) How many **100g** weights are in **500g**? _____

3) How many **50g** weights are in **250g**? _____

4) How many **250g** weights are in **500g**? _____

5) How many **250g** weights are in **3kg**? _____

6) How many **500g** weights are in **3kg**? _____

7) How many **50g** weights are in **500g**? _____

8) How many **500g** weights are in **1kg**? _____

9) How many **100g** weights are in **1kg**? _____

10) How many **250g** weights are in **2kg**? _____

Score

Example: What weights will make the scales balance?

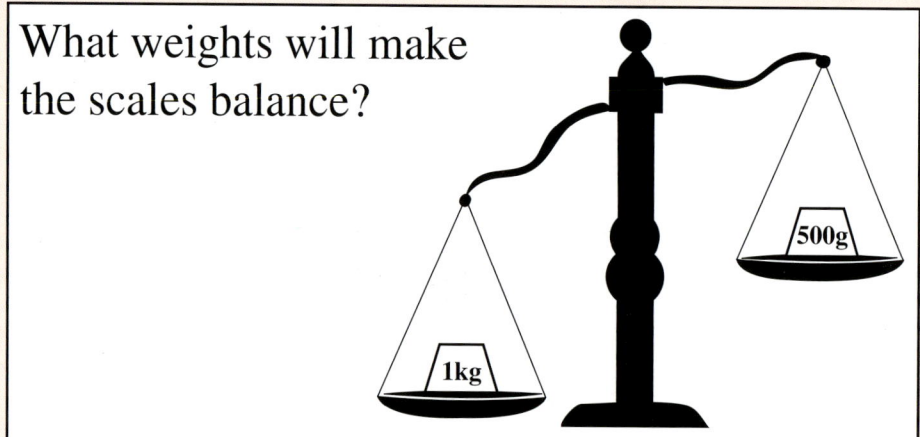

Step 1 - The lower side of the scales is the heavier side and weighs **1kg**.

Step 2 - The higher and lighter side weighs **500g**.

Step 3 - Subtract to find the difference between the two sides. **1kg − 500g = 500g**

Step 4 - Starting with the largest possible weight, work out which weights will make up **500g**. This is **500g**.

Answer: **500g**

Exercise 10: 15

What weights will make the scales balance?

1) [250g on lower left; 100g, 100g on higher right]

2) [500g on lower left; 250g on higher right]

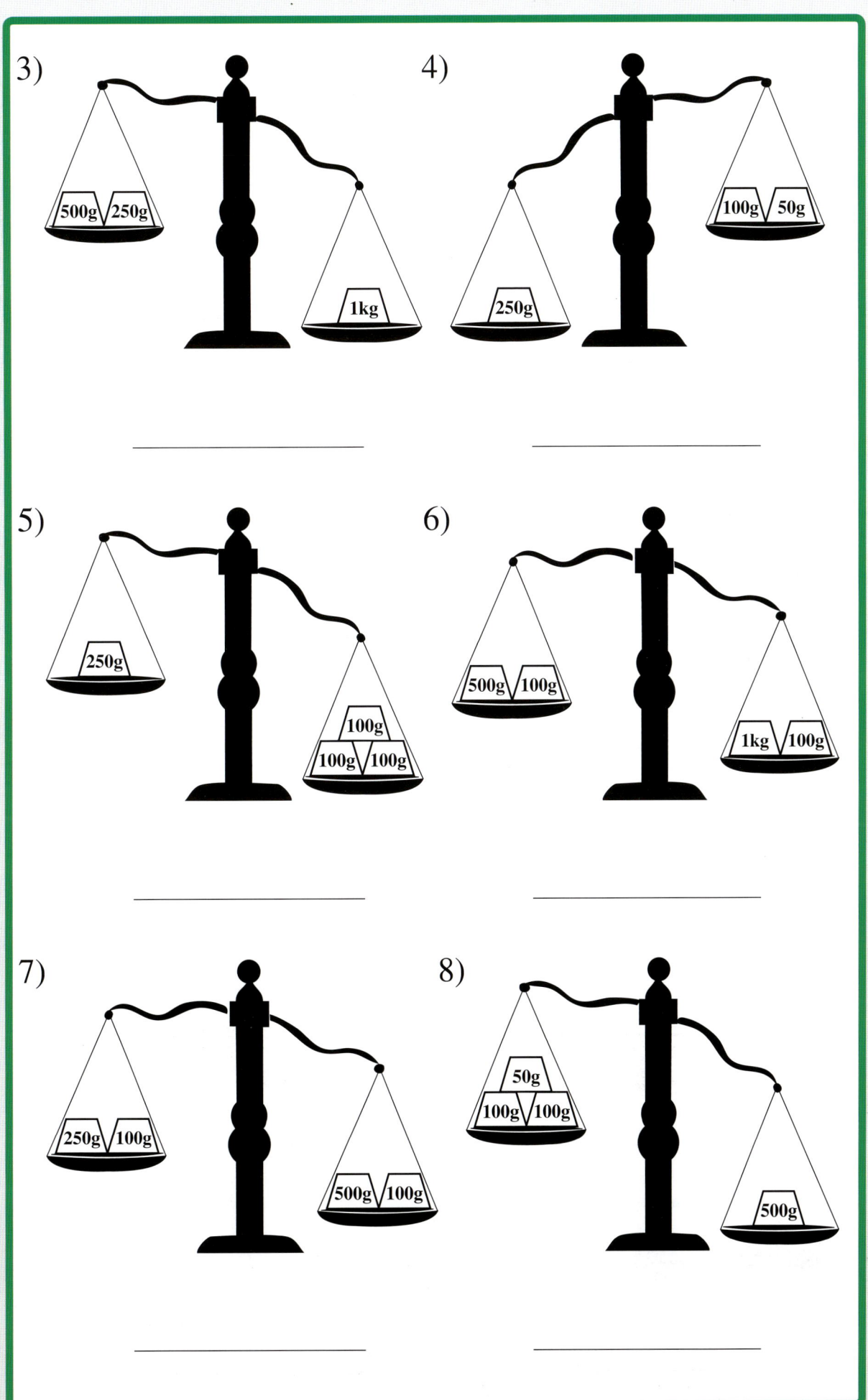

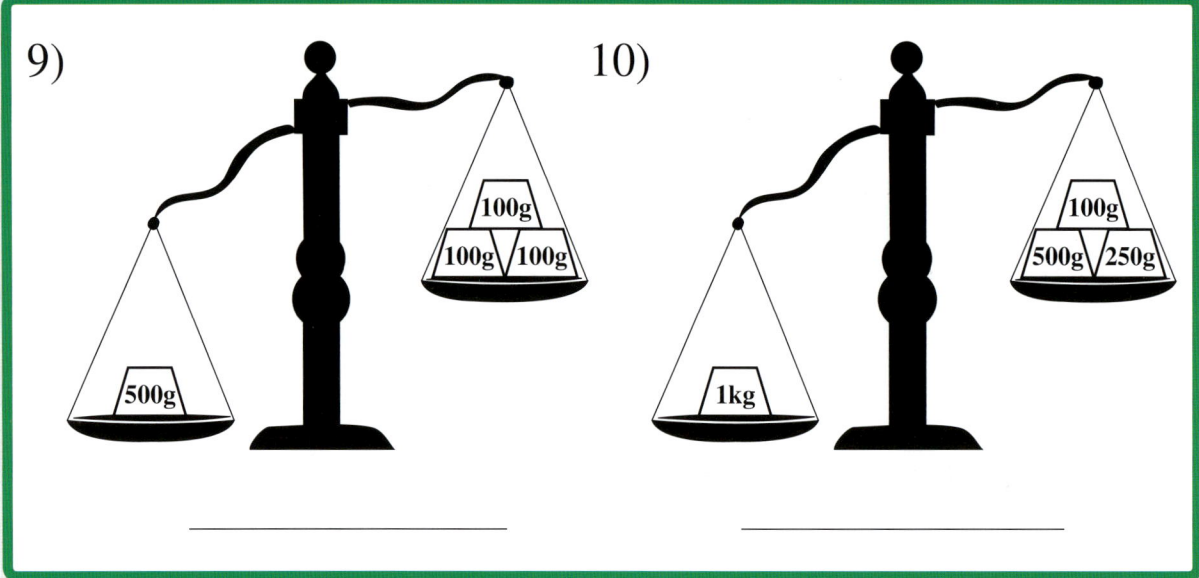

5. Greater Than or Smaller Than

When comparing the size of measurements it is best to convert everything to the smallest unit of measurement. This means mostly whole numbers are being compared.

Example: Put the correct sign (> or <) between $\frac{1}{4}\ell$ and **240mℓ**.

Step 1 - Change the fraction of a litre to millilitres.
$\frac{1}{4}\ell$ is **250mℓ**.

Step 2 - Compare the size of the measurements in millilitres.
250mℓ > 240mℓ

Change the amounts back to their original forms.
This means $\frac{1}{4}\ell$ is larger than **240mℓ**.

Answer: $\frac{1}{4}\ell$ > **240mℓ**

Exercise 10: 16   Answer the following:

1) Which is longer, **8cm** or **75mm**? _____
2) Which is heavier, **2.3kg** or **2,250g**? _____

3) Which is heavier, $1\frac{1}{4}$kg or **1,300g**? _____

4) Which is longer, **1.75m** or **180cm**? _____

Put the correct sign (> or <) between the following amounts:

5) $\frac{3}{4}\ell$ **760mℓ** 6) **1km and 200m** **1.5km**

7) **4,800mm** **4.75m** 8) **510mℓ** $\frac{1}{2}\ell$

9) **1,600g** $1\frac{1}{2}$kg 10) **13mm** **1.4cm**

6. Metric Calculations

Metric Calculations can include any of the Four Rules of Number: addition, subtraction, multiplication or division.

Example: Multiply **1.47ℓ** by **3**.

Mulitply using standard short decimal multiplication.

Answer: **4.41ℓ**

```
  1 . 4 7
      3 ×
  ───────
  4 . 4 1
    1   2
```

Exercise 10: 17 Calculate the following:

Score

1) **5.2m + 1.75m + 1.5m** 2) **898mℓ – 358mℓ**

```
   5 . 2 0 m
   1 . 7 5 m
   1 . 5 0 m +
   ─────────
```

```
   8 9 8 m$\ell$
   3 5 8 m$\ell$ –
   ─────────
```

3) **1.5t × 2**   4) **450m*l* ÷ 2**

×
———
———

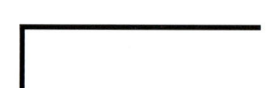

5) **823g + 150g + 604g**   6) **908mm − 125mm**

+   −
———   ———
———   ———

7) **58cm × 3**   8) **5.25km ÷ 5**

×
———
———

9) **3.6*l* + 2.1*l* + 0.25*l***   10) **100kg ÷ 10**

+
———
———

7. Estimating Measurements

An **Estimation** or **Approximation** is a sensible guess. It is not based on a calculation, but on a knowledge of the rough measurement of everyday items.

The symbol ≈ means 'roughly equal to' and it is often used in estimating questions.

The following measures are useful guides for estimating:

Length

15cm ≈ The length of a pencil.

30cm ≈ An A4 piece of paper lengthways.

1m ≈ The width of a single bed.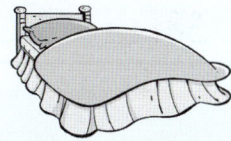

Weight

500g ≈ A can of beans.

1kg ≈ A bag of sugar.

Capacity

250mℓ ≈ A mug of tea.

330mℓ ≈ A can of drink.

1ℓ ≈ A large carton of juice.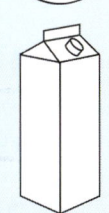

Example: What is the approximate weight of a hamster?
   40ℓ   0.6mm   1kg   120g   200mℓ

Step 1 - Rule out amounts that use the wrong unit of measurement.

   40ℓ and **200mℓ** both measure capacity.

   0.6mm measures distance.

Step 2 - Select the closest estimation from the table that could be used to estimate the weight of a hamster.

   500g ≈ A can of beans

   A hamster will weigh less than a can of beans, so look for an amount that is less than **500g**.

   1kg is too big, so it must be **120g**.

   ~~40ℓ~~   ~~0.6mm~~   ~~1kg~~   120g   ~~200mℓ~~
   capacity   distance   too big   capcity

   Answer: **120g**

Exercise 10: 18   Answer the following:

1) What is the approximate weight of a bag of flour?

   2.5cm   1kg   100g   150mℓ   1.5m   _____

2) What is the approximate height of a bookcase?

   100mℓ   1.75m   20cm   5kg   2ℓ   _____

3) What is the approximate capacity of a teapot?

   100g   750mℓ   1.1ℓ   325m   1.2km   _____

4) What is the approximate length of a paintbrush?

   20g   1ℓ   15cm   1m   1kg   _____

5) What is the approximate width of a rubber?

   10kg 5mm 10cm 300ml 500g _____

6) What is the approximate capacity of a cup of tea?

   200g 250ml 2l 350m 20cm _____

7) What is the approximate weight of a packet of sweets?

   150m 2kg 30ml 1l 45g _____

8) What is the approximate length of a pencil?

   2m 100ml 16cm 350g 2kg _____

9) What is the approximate height of a tree?

   30cm 100g 12m 250ml 2kg _____

10) What is the approximate weight of a can of carrots?

   100m 4kg 300g 25cm 1l _____

8. Temperature

Temperature is the measurement of how hot or cold something is. It is most commonly used to describe how hot or cold the air is in a particular place.

Temperature is measured using a thermometer in degrees Celcius (°C).

Water boils at **100°C** and freezes at **0°C**.

Temperature measurements can be either **Positive** or **Negative**, in the same way as on this number line:

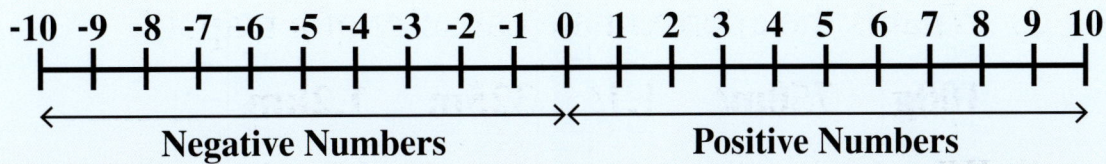

Negative numbers are used to show very cold temperatures below **0°C** (**zero**).

Example: What temperature is shown on the thermometer?

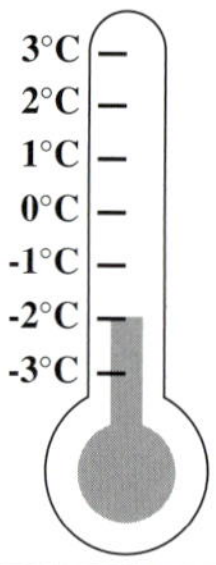

The liquid level in the thermometer rests at **-2°C** meaning that is the temperature.

Answer: **-2°C**

Exercise 10: 19

What temperature is shown on the thermometer?

Score

1) 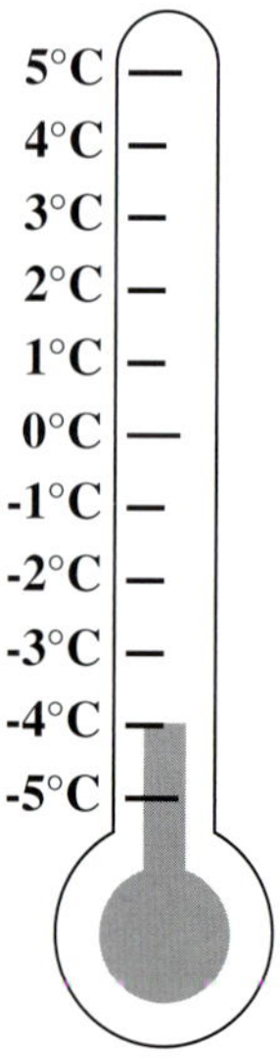
2) 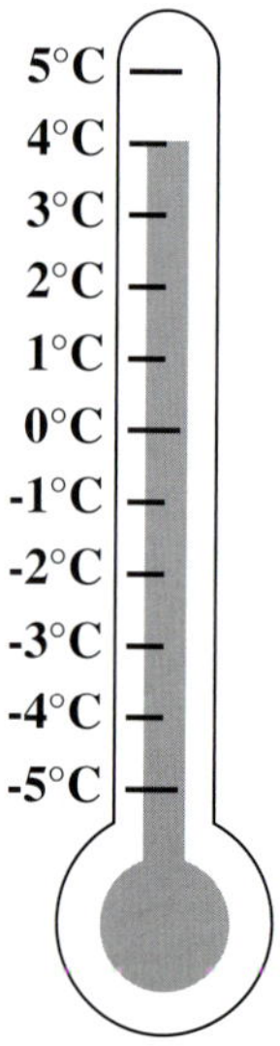
3) 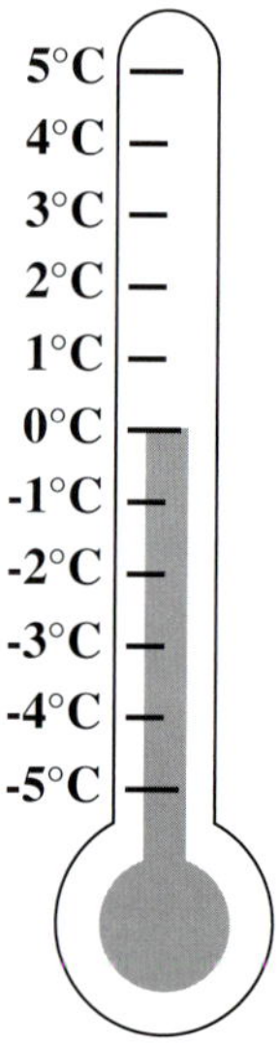
4) 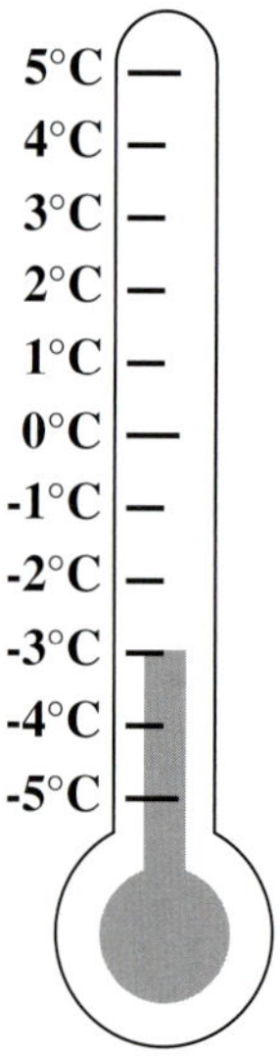
5) 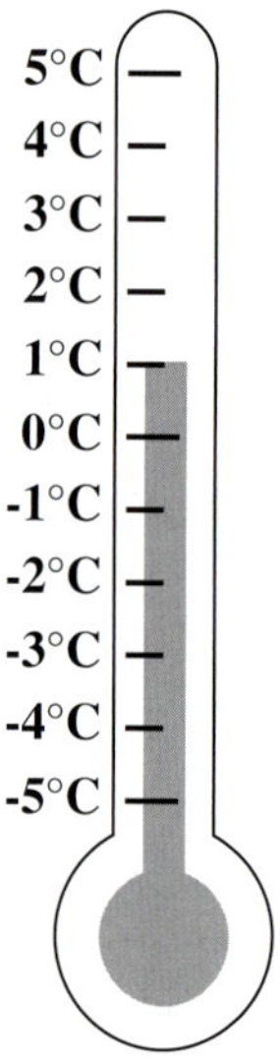
6)

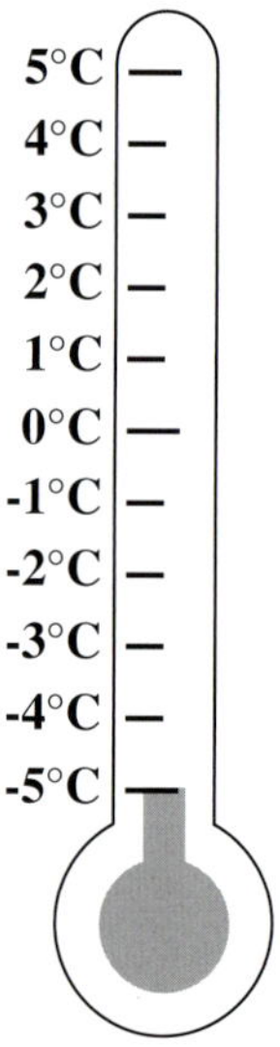

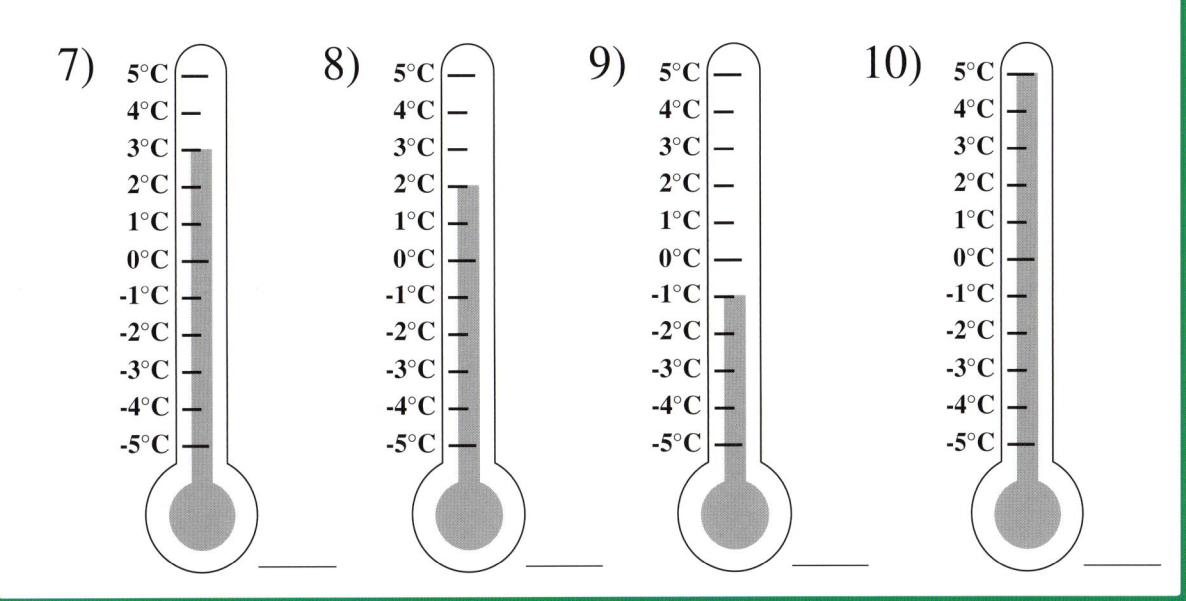

9. Problem Solving

Example: Stuart ran in a **1,000m** race. He got a stitch after running **227m**. How far did Stuart still have to run?

Subtract the distances to find how far Stuart still had to run.

1,000m − 227m = 773m

$$\begin{array}{r} {}^{0}\cancel{1}{}^{9}\cancel{0}{}^{9}\cancel{0}\,0 \\ 0\,2\,2\,7\,- \\ \hline 0\,7\,7\,3 \end{array}$$

Answer: **773m**

Exercise 10: 20   Answer the following:

Score

1) A piece of ribbon is **3cm** longer than **15cm** and **3cm** shorter than **21cm**. How long is it? _____

2) Finola wants to make a birthday cake. If a tablespoon of sugar weighs **25g** and the recipe requires **100g**, how many tablespoons does she need? _____

3) Anil runs in a **400m** race. His leg starts to hurt after **117m**. How far does he still have to run? _____

4) To get to the playground, James has to walk **325** metres and Katie has to walk **17** metres more. How far does Katie have to walk? _____

5) What is the difference in height between the drawings of these two bottles? _____

6) Jonah wants to make some cakes for a bake sale. The recipe requires **150g** of sugar for **10** cakes. He has been asked to make **30** cakes. How much sugar does he need? _____

7) If **2ℓ** of lemonade cost **£2**, how much does **4ℓ** cost? _____

8) Nicole needs to buy some milk for her family of five for a week. Which of these is the most sensible amount?

   10m   3kg   200mℓ   300g   7ℓ _____

9) There are **500g** of sweets in a bowl to give out at a party. If $\frac{1}{2}$ of the sweets are given out, what is the weight of the leftover sweets? _____

10) A **four-person** relay team is running a **1,000m** race. Each person runs $\frac{1}{4}$ of the **1,000m** distance. How far does each person run? _____

Chapter Eleven
AVERAGES

Data is a collection of numbers or amounts that have been grouped together for the purpose of study.

The **Average** is a general term used to describe the middle, or central, value of a group of data. There are three methods for finding this value:

Mode • **Median** • **Mean** (often called the **Average**)

It is possible to also find the **Range** of a group of data. This is the difference between the smallest and largest amounts in the group of data.

1. Mode

Mode is the number that appears the most times or most often in a group of numbers. It gives a rough idea of the central value.

Example: Find the mode of these numbers:
3 9 1 2 4 3 9 5 3

Step 1 - Rearrange the numbers in size order.

1 2 3 3 3 4 5 9 9

Step 2 - Count the numbers to check all of them have been used. There are 9 numbers.

Step 3 - Select the number that appears most often. This is the mode.

1 2 3 3 3 4 5 9 9

Answer: The mode is **3**.

Exercise 11: 1 Calculate the mode:

Score

1) **43   18   45   19   18   6   2**   Mode: _____

2) **56   13   43   27   77   43   18**   Mode: _____

3) **51   21   16   44   21   95   21**   Mode: _____

4) **2   31   20   1   5   1   16   1**   Mode: _____

5) **30   21   73   65   30   21   30**   Mode: _____

6) **82   61   61   40   71   61   38**   Mode: _____

7) **50   18   20   43   20   18   20**   Mode: _____

8) **74   57   32   53   57   87   57**   Mode: _____

9) **4   37   6   36   6   36   44   6**   Mode: _____

10) **11   89   44   68   44   89   44**   Mode: _____

2. Median

The **Median** is the number that lies in the middle of a sorted group of numbers. It gives a rough idea of the central value.

Example: Find the median of these numbers:
9   4   2   8   1   8   7   1   9

Step 1 - Rearrange the numbers in size order.
      1   1   2   4   7   8   8   9   9

Step 2 - Count the numbers to check all of them have been used. There are 9 numbers.

Step 3 - Select the number that appears exactly in the middle.
This is the median.

1   1   2   4 |7| 8   8   9   9
   ←——————   ——————→
 Four numbers this side.   Four numbers this side.

Answer: The median is **7**.

Exercise 11: 2   Calculate the median:

Score

1) 18   24   85   63   4   Median: _____

2) 10   63   13   88   79   Median: _____

3) 42   74   66   19   84   Median: _____

4) 10   48   59   74   50   Median: _____

5) 98   61   95   76   51   6   10   Median: _____

6) 24   63   21   57   79   13   80   Median: _____

7) 8   38   13   48   63   22   39   Median: _____

8) 83   22   11   74   34   31   46   Median: _____

9) 70   58   55   99   9   2   6   Median: _____

10) 63   27   58   29   8   15   34   Median: _____

3. Range

The **Range** is the distance between the smallest and the largest number in a sorted group of numbers.

Example: Find the range of these numbers:
4 6 7 3 8 9 4 7 5

Step 1 - Rearrange the numbers in size order.
3 4 4 5 6 7 7 8 9

Step 2 - Count the numbers to check all of them have been used. There are 9 numbers.

Step 3 - Subtract the smallest number from the largest number to find the range.
3 4 4 5 6 7 7 8 9
9 – 3 = 6
This is the range.
Answer: The range is **6**.

Exercise 11: 3   Calculate the range:

Score

1) 42 57 19 76 34   Range: _____

2) 41 77 7 36 16   Range: _____

3) 34 46 63 68 36   Range: _____

4) 26 40 9 86 19 21   Range: _____

5) 9 29 94 56 47 35   Range: _____

6) 42 83 86 77 3 78   Range: _____

7) 94 12 15 61 14 37   Range: _____

8) 55 70 69 38 43 31 61 Range: _____

9) 3 70 60 97 53 13 25   Range: _____

10) 75 66 12 15 67 1 93 Range: _____

4. The 'Mean' or Average

The **Mean** is the **Average** of a group of numbers. It gives an accurate middle value. It is calculated by adding all the amounts together and then dividing the total by the number of amounts.

Mean = Total of all the items ÷ Number of items

For example, the average of **3**, **7** and **2** is **4**.

If the calculation **3 + 7 + 2 = 12** were 'evened out' it would be **4 + 4 + 4 = 12**, which gives the same answer.

Example: Find the mean of these numbers:
5 2 6 2 1 3 1 4 3

Step 1 - Add all of the numbers together to find the total.
5 + 2 + 6 + 2 + 1 + 3 + 1 + 4 + 3 = 27

Step 2 - Count how many numbers there are to find the number of items. There are **9** items.

Step 3 - Divide the total by the number of items.
27 ÷ 9 = 3

Answer: The mean is **3**.

Exercise 11: 4   Calculate the mean:

1) 19 11 3   Mean: _____
2) 4 3 14   Mean: _____
3) 14 17 11   Mean: _____

4) 5 10 12   Mean: _____
5) 1 5 3   Mean: _____
6) 5 7 9 15   Mean: _____
7) 20 2 5 13   Mean: _____
8) 16 12 3 9   Mean: _____
9) 19 8 9 1 13   Mean: _____
10) 11 20 13 9 2   Mean: _____

5. Problem Solving

Exercise 11: 5 Answer the following:

Score

1) Tom reads an average of **10** pages a week. His book is **50** pages long. How many weeks will it take him to read it? _____

The temperatures recorded over a week were:

Day	Monday	Tuesday	Wednesday	Thursday	Friday
Temperature	7°C	4°C	7°C	10°C	7°C

What was the:

2) mode? _____   3) median? _____
4) range? _____   5) mean? _____

Jayden works in an animal sanctuary. He records how

Week 1	Week 2	Week 3	Week 4	Week 5
20	13	12	12	18

many animals arrive each week. What is the:

6) mode? _____   7) median? _____
8) range? _____   9) mean? _____

10) The total cost of **three** drinks is **£3.60**. What is the mean cost? _____

Answers

Key Stage 2 Maths
Year 3/4 Workbook 6

Chapter Nine
Money & Costs
Exercise 9: 1
1) 5p
2) 199p
3) 519p
4) 176p
5) 230p
6) 45p
7) 238p
8) 120p
9) 351p
10) 424p

Exercise 9: 2
1) £8.36
2) £1.50
3) £2.99
4) £0.25
5) £1.22
6) £3.08
7) £5.31
8) £1.83
9) £0.74
10) £0.10

Exercise 9: 3
1) 1 pound and 53 pence
2) 0 pounds and 41 pence
3) 2 pounds and 79 pence
4) 5 pounds and 63 pence
5) 0 pounds and 98 pence
6) 3 pounds and 25 pence
7) 1 pound and 81 pence
8) 0 pounds and 67 pence
9) 2 pounds and 30 pence
10) 1 pound and 7 pence

Exercise 9: 4
1) £2.84
2) £1.26
3) £0.56
4) £4.75
5) £1.03
6) £1.80
7) £0.90
8) £5.14
9) £3.32
10) £0.01

Exercise 9: 5
1) <
2) >
3) >
4) <
5) <
6) >
7) <
8) >
9) >
10) <

Exercise 9: 6
1) £2.50
2) £1.28
3) £1.50
4) £2.30
5) £0.13 or 13p
6) £0.29 or 29p
7) £1.22
8) £0.42 or 42p
9) £0.34 or 34p
10) £3.70

Exercise 9: 7
1) 5p
2) 1p
3) 2p
4) 5p
5) 2p

73

Key Stage 2 Maths
Year 3/4 Workbook 6

Answers

6) 10p
7) 20p
8) 10p
9) 2p
10) 5p

Exercise 9: 8
1) 20p, 5p, 2p, 1p,
2) 10p, 2p, 1p
3) 20p, 20p, 10p
4) 20p, 20p, 5p, 1p
5) 20p, 10p, 2p
6) 20p, 5p, 2p
7) £1, 50p, 20p, 5p
8) 20p, 10p, 10p
9) £2, 10p, 5p, 1p
10) £1, 20p, 5p

Exercise 9: 9
1) £1, 1p
2) 50p, 20p, 5p
3) £2, 50p
4) £1, 50p, 20p, 10p
5) £2, £2, 5p, 2p, 1p
6) £2, £2, £1, 5p
7) 50p, 20p, 10p, 2p, 1p
8) 50p, 20p, 20p, 5p, 2p, 1p
9) £2, £1, 50p, 20p, 10p, 5p, 2p, 1p
10) £2, £1, 10p, 2p

Exercise 9: 10
1) 18p
2) 87p
3) 44p
4) 71p
5) 99p
6) 6p
7) 40p
8) 42p
9) 65p
10) 52p

Exercise 9: 11
1) £3.82
2) £4.54
3) £2.97
4) £2.25
5) £1.75
6) £4.13
7) £3.30
8) £0.85 or 85p
9) £1.50
10) £4.08

Exercise 9: 12
1) 50p, 20p, 2p, 2p
2) 20p, 10p, 5p
3) 50p, 10p, 2p
4) 50p, 20p, 20p, 5p, 2p
5) £1, 20p, 2p
6) 20p, 20p, 5p, 1p
7) £2, 20p, 10p, 2p, 1p
8) £1, 50p, 5p, 2p, 2p
9) £2, £2, 10p, 2p, 1p
10) £1, 50p, 10p, 5p, 2p, 1p

Exercise 9: 13
1) 49p
2) 81p
3) 67p
4) 73p
5) 27p
6) 77p
7) 81p
8) 90p
9) 76p
10) 96p

Exercise 9: 14
1) £6.55
2) £30.93
3) £12.48
4) £18.68
5) £13.75

Answers

Key Stage 2 Maths
Year 3/4 Workbook 6

6) £2.54
7) £49.19
8) £14.40
9) £2.70
10) £25.97

Exercise 9: 15
1) 34p
2) 76p
3) 42p
4) 49p
5) 9p
6) 13p
7) 68p
8) 73p
9) 43p
10) 23p

Exercise 9: 16
1) £0.75
2) £6.08
3) £9.49
4) £21.77
5) £5.67
6) £3.07
7) £16.91
8) £11.87
9) £11.11
10) £24.14

Exercise 9: 17
1) 12p
2) £1 or 100p
3) 70p
4) 5p
5) 60p
6) 9p
7) 80p
8) 6p
9) 40p
10) 50p

Exercise 9: 18
1) £2.28
2) £1.26
3) £1.15
4) £1.84
5) £2.66
6) £2.28
7) £2.40
8) £7.29
9) £0.72
10) £4.55

Exercise 9: 19
1) £25.68
2) £5.37
3) £14.32
4) £62.23
5) £9.18
6) £33.42
7) £19.80
8) £20.19
9) £19.28
10) £49.95

Exercise 9: 20
1) 11
2) 8
3) 8
4) 11
5) 8
6) 3
7) 5
8) 4
9) 2
10) 2

Exercise 9: 21
1) 21p
2) 12p
3) 19p
4) 34p
5) 11p

6) 14p
7) 17p
8) 16p
9) 14p
10) 11p

Exercise 9: 22
1) 10
2) 15
3) 30
4) 35
5) 8
6) 4
7) 10
8) 40
9) 50
10) 20

Exercise 9: 23
1) £0.37
2) £1.53
3) £0.75
4) £0.98
5) £3.75
6) £0.54
7) £1.64
8) £1.34
9) £0.92
10) £2.34

Exercise 9: 24
1) 48p
2) 34p
3) 90p
4) 5p
5) £2 or 200p
6) 48p
7) £1.60 or 160p
8) £2.15 or 215p
9) 8p
10) 71p

© 2016 Stephen Curran

Key Stage 2 Maths
Year 3/4 Workbook 6

Answers

Exercise 9: 25
1) 9
2) £9.75
3) 10
4) £2
5) £4.56
6) 72p
7) 8
8) £105
9) £20.97
10) £15.20

Exercise 9: 26
1) £4.74
2) £1.75
3) £30
4) £2.90
5) £6.25
6) £2.12
7) 80p
8) £1.72
9) £1
10) £1.20

Chapter Ten
Measurement

Exercise 10: 1
1) 5,000m
2) 40mm
3) 3m
4) 7cm
5) 2cm
6) 8km
7) 1m
8) 900cm
9) 6m
10) 1,000m

Exercise 10: 2

1-10)

More than **1m**	Less than **1m**
Car	Book
Ship	Cup
Sheep	Juice Carton
Adult (Height)	Microwave
Building	Sweet

Exercise 10: 3
1) cm
2) m
3) cm or m
4) cm
5) km
6) mm
7) cm
8) mm
9) km
10) cm

Exercise 10: 4
1) 8,000g
2) 5kg
3) 2,000g
4) 7kg
5) 6kg
6) 9kg
7) 4,000g
8) 1kg
9) 3kg
10) 1t

Exercise 10: 5

1-10)

More than **1kg**	Less than **1kg**
Tree	Toothpaste
Lorry	Shoe
Heavy Rucksack	Feather
Seagull	Can of Beans
Aeroplane	Balloon

Answers

Key Stage 2 Maths
Year 3/4 Workbook 6

Exercise 10: 6
1) t
2) g
3) g
4) kg
5) t
6) g
7) kg
8) kg
9) g
10) t

Exercise 10: 7
1) 1ℓ
2) 7ℓ
3) 6,000mℓ
4) 8,000mℓ
5) 10,000mℓ
6) 2,000mℓ
7) 4ℓ
8) 9ℓ
9) 5ℓ
10) 3,000mℓ

Exercise 10: 8
1)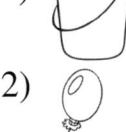
2)
3)
4)
5)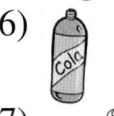
6)
7)

8)
9) Trophy
10) Vase

Exercise 10: 9
1) ℓ
2) mℓ
3) mℓ
4) ℓ
5) mℓ
6) mℓ or ℓ
7) mℓ
8) ℓ
9) mℓ or ℓ
10) mℓ

Exercise 10: 10
1) 5mm
2) 250mℓ
3) 500g
4) 50cm
5) 750mm
6) 250g
7) 500mℓ
8) 500m
9) 25cm
10) 750m

Exercise 10: 11
1) 6cm and 5mm
2) 1km and 750m
3) 3kg and 250g
4) 2kg and 500g
5) 8m and 50cm
6) 5ℓ and 250mℓ
7) 4ℓ and 750mℓ
8) 7m and 50cm
9) 9kg and 200g
10) 1t and 250kg

Exercise 10: 12
1) 1.5kg
2) 3.25m
3) 9.75ℓ
4) 7.25km
5) 4.5cm
6) 2.5cm
7) 5.75ℓ
8) 6.25m
9) 1.75km
10) 8.25kg

Exercise 10: 13
1) 8mm
2) 3.2cm
3) 55mm
4) 7.3cm
5) 4.5cm or 45mm
6) 5.6cm or 56mm
7) 5.4cm or 54mm
8) 8.8cm or 88mm
9) 3.2cm or 32mm
10) 7.5cm or 75mm

Exercise 10: 14
1) 2
2) 5
3) 5
4) 2
5) 12
6) 6
7) 10
8) 2
9) 10
10) 8

Exercise 10: 15
1) 50g
2) 250g
3) 250g
4) 100g
5) 50g

Key Stage 2 Maths
Year 3/4 Workbook 6

Answers

6) 500g
7) 250g
8) 250g
9) 100g, 100g
10) 100g, 50g

Exercise 10: 16
1) 8cm
2) 2.3kg
3) 1,300g
4) 180cm
5) <
6) <
7) >
8) >
9) >
10) <

Exercise 10: 17
1) 8.45m
2) 540mℓ
3) 3t
4) 225mℓ
5) 1,577g
6) 783mm
7) 174cm
8) 1.05km
9) 5.95ℓ
10) 10kg

Exercise 10: 18
1) 1kg
2) 1.75m
3) 1.1ℓ
4) 15cm
5) 5mm
6) 250mℓ
7) 45g
8) 16cm
9) 12m
10) 300g

Exercise 10: 19
1) -4°C
2) 4°C
3) 0°C
4) -3°C
5) 1°C
6) -5°C
7) 3°C
8) 2°C
9) -1°C
10) 5°C

Exercise 10: 20
1) 18cm
2) 4
3) 283m
4) 342m
5) 1.5cm or 15mm
6) 450g
7) £4
8) 7ℓ
9) 250g
10) 250m

Chapter Eleven
Averages

Exercise 11: 1
1) 18
2) 43
3) 21
4) 1
5) 30
6) 61
7) 20
8) 57
9) 6
10) 44

Exercise 11: 2
1) 24
2) 63
3) 66
4) 50

5) 61
6) 57
7) 38
8) 34
9) 55
10) 29

Exercise 11: 3
1) 57
2) 70
3) 34
4) 77
5) 85
6) 83
7) 82
8) 39
9) 94
10) 92

Exercise 11: 4
1) 11
2) 7
3) 14
4) 9
5) 3
6) 9
7) 10
8) 10
9) 10
10) 11

Exercise 11: 5
1) 5
2) 7°C
3) 7°C
4) 6°C
5) 7°C
6) 12
7) 13
8) 8
9) 15
10) £1.20

PROGRESS CHARTS

Shade in your score for each exercise on the graph. Add up for your total score.

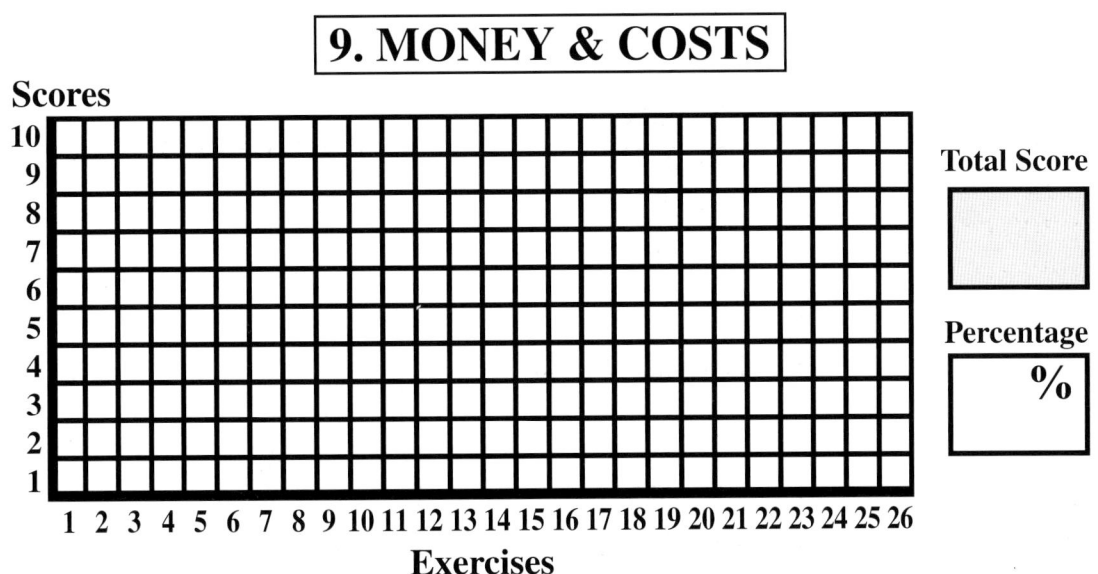

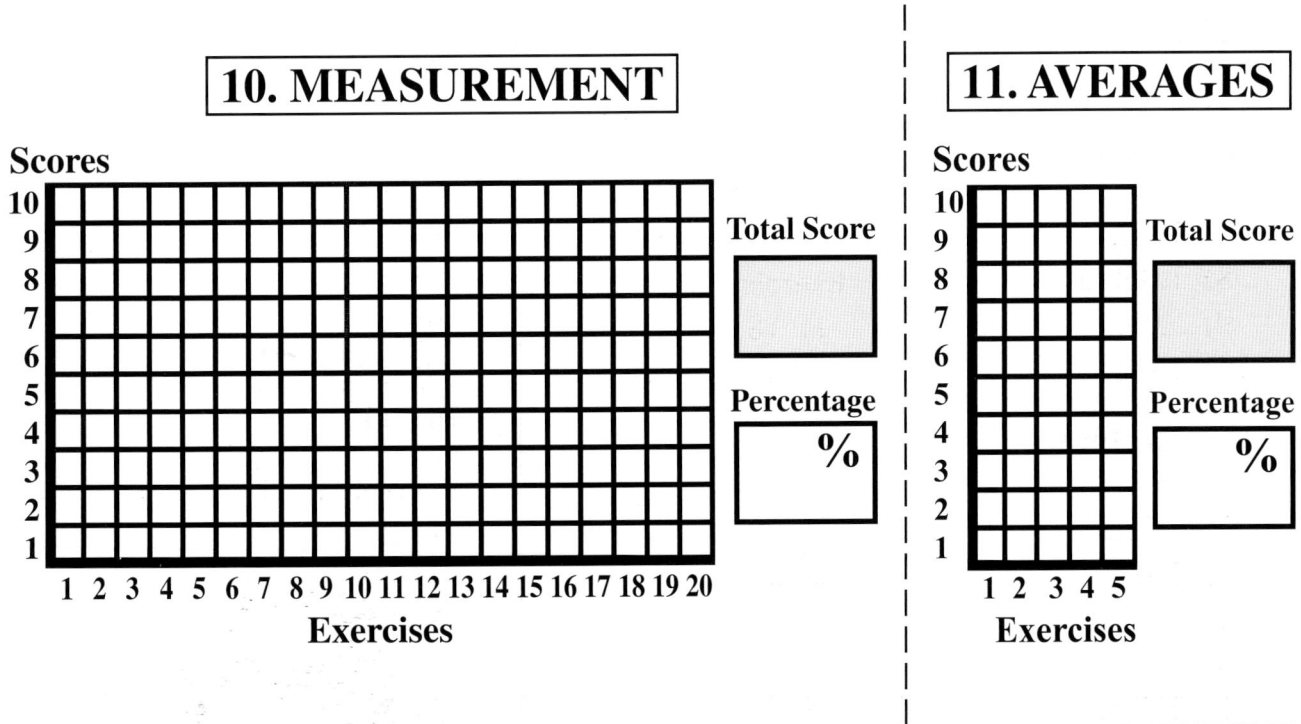

Overall Percentage [%   ]

CERTIFICATE OF
ACHIEVEMENT

This certifies

_____

has successfully completed

Key Stage 2 Maths
Year 3/4
WORKBOOK 6

Overall percentage score achieved ☐ %

Comment _____

_____

Signed _____
(teacher/parent/guardian)

Date _____